THE
QUEEN
MOTHER

First English edition published by Colour Library Books Ltd.
© 1983 Illustrations: Keystone Press Agency, London.
© 1983 Text: Colour Library Books Ltd., Guildford, Surrey, England.
This edition published by Greenwich House, a division of Arlington
House Inc., distributed by Crown Publishers, Inc.
h g f e d c b a
Display and text filmsetting by Acesetters Ltd., Richmond, Surrey, England.
Printed and bound in Barcelona, Spain. by Cayfosa and Eurobinder.
All rights reserved
ISBN 0 517 429799

THE
QUEEN
MOTHER

GREENWICH HOUSE

The Queen Mother

The humble fish-bone has rarely achieved the distinction of becoming remotely notorious, though there are stories enough to link some of the more wretched and unassuming objects of every-day life with phenomenal influences on the course of world history. Cleopatra's asp, Robert the Bruce's spider and Sir Isaac Newton's apple have all been credited with an assured place in the annals of man. Late one Sunday evening in November 1982, these and other historical catalysts were emulated by a fish-bone which lodged in the throat of none other than Queen Elizabeth the Queen Mother during a party at Royal Lodge Windsor where Her Majesty was entertaining a group of family and friends to dinner.

The sight of this gathering of eminent worthies doing their best to slap the offending foreign body from the royal gullet must have been less than dignified, and all concerned will be grateful that the incident took place in private rather than in public. The sheer panic which must at times have seized the guests at the thought that their attempts might prove fruitless, and that the life of one of Britain's most august citizens might be in serious danger must have been positively unspeakable. Ultimately the Queen Mother's physician, Dr John Clayton, was called in and, after consultation with the Queen's physician, Dr John Batten, it was decided to commit the royal victim to hospital and, not for the first time in her life, she was driven up to London to be admitted for an operation. She was accompanied on this occasion by Princess Margaret, her younger daughter and one of her guests that evening, who stayed at the hospital during the course of the operation.

The hospital – King Edward VII's Hospital for Officers, in Marylebone – received its unexpected patient at 1.30 in the morning, and the operation which took place shortly afterwards proved comparatively simple and certainly successful. As on every other occasion when she has attended the hospital in the past, the Queen Mother proved a model patient, and almost scorned the great public concern for her well-being by discharging herself a day earlier than everyone expected. "For a woman of her age", said one of the hospital staff, "her constitution is quite remarkable. After coming round from the anaesthetic, she was bubbling and cheerful for the rest of her stay".

With hindsight the entire episode, though it lasted only two days, seems to have provoked a most disproportionate amount of popular attention - the sort that keeps the ear glued to the radio and the eye casting around for the latest newspaper headline or bill-board. The crowds which gathered outside the hospital and the never-ending telephone calls to Clarence House throughout the period of public knowledge of the crisis may appear to have given the incident an undue degree of significance. Of course, that is a question of priorities, and for a nation beset by one of the biggest post-war depressions and in the grip of almost unprecedented unemployment, the minutiae of a fairly routine, if emergency operation on a Queen Dowager may not rank as being of earth-shattering importance. What the commotion did display, however, was the degree and spontaneity of what King George V rather bashfully acknowledged as the "love" of ordinary people – and the media who exist to feed them their information – for this most rewarding of royal figures, and the feeling that because her weekly appearances in public have of late fallen far behind those of most other members of her family in number, she has been taken rather too much for granted. It was, after all, ironically telling that on the day of her admission to hospital, the results of a poll taken by a reputable firm of researchers into popular opinion was published, in which the Queen Mother herself was rated best at carrying out public duties.

Her Majesty's emergence from hospital on 23rd November helped put things right: the full weight of London's press and broadcasting media were on the spot to welcome her, along with some three hundred vociferous well-wishers. For her part, she stood cheerfully on the threshold acknowledging the public acclaim with her now legendary smile, her customary sheer enjoyment of a little bit of good natured fuss, and above all the time and the will to reward the patience of the photographers with the opportunity to obtain photographs that would please any picture desk editor. It was even possible to suspect that amid the gratitude for the successful outcome of an incident which could have gone horribly wrong, the Queen Mother was rather enjoying the mischievous twist of fate which had suddenly steered the nation's glance towards her presence.

Much is made of Queen Elizabeth's Scottish ancestry but it is pedantically a falsehood to say that she is a Scottish Queen. She was born no more than thirty miles from London in a house at St Paul's Walden Bury, near Hatfield in Hertfordshire. Built by Sir William Chambers in the mid-eighteenth century it was and is a small mansion of warm red brick, set on rising ground, even now enjoying the tranquility – rare in an area shot through with motorways – afforded by massive, ancient trees, thick woods and vast expanses of lawn, where the battle to keep the daisies down has long since been conceded. It was the weekend retreat of the then Lord and Lady Glamis from their London House, 20 St James's Square where, since they took it on lease in 1906, they lived for most of the year. But for three or four months, after the London season ended, the family moved up to Scotland to spend the late summer and autumn at Glamis Castle, "heavy with atmosphere" as one of its guests described it in 1922, "sinister, lugubrious . . . Redolent with the macabre legends of Macbeth, Duncan and Malcolm II.

The Queen Mother

Lady Elizabeth's childhood spent, during the glorious twilight of the Edwardian Era, with her beloved brother David, was one of happiness and enjoyment. But it was soon to be brought to a sudden end. On the night of August 4th 1914, Lady Elizabeth's fourteenth birthday, the news of the outbreak of World War reached London. By the end of that week Lady Elizabeth was travelling north to begin "those awful four years that followed" at Glamis, but even here, up to eight hundred miles from the theatre of war she was not immune from its effects. Within three months of the Declaration, part of Glamis Castle became a convalescent hospital for wounded soldiers, the dining room was converted into a sixteen-bed ward run by Lady Strathmore's third daughter, Rose, who was undergoing training as a nurse. Lady Strathmore herself was there to supervise and, even at the tender age of fourteen, Lady Elizabeth was a willing recruit as, in December 1914 the first of fifteen hundred casualties arrived in khaki uniforms or in the dull blue garb of the hospitals from which they were being transferred. Without qualifications save those of charm, sympathy and helpfulness, she warmed to the possibilities of this unexpected turn of events: she took her meals with the wounded visitors, helped them to write letters home, did their shopping for them, played cards and billiards with them, distributed their mail and even brought small persents for them – in short, she played the junior hostess. In addition there were other activities in support of the War effort – public ones, like the manning of stalls during sales of work, and private ones including, like Sister Susie of the tongue-twisting song, sewing shirts for soldiers.

The London Season habit was not slow in returning after the cessation of hostilities, even though the uncertain and self-conscious resumption of everyday life muted the brilliance of the palmier pre-War days, and the youngest of the Strathmore girls now took full advantage. She returned to London for the great occasions, such as Royal Ascot and, in July, the National Victory March, and for the more relaxed social enjoyments like parties, receptions and society weddings. It was the year of her social *début*, her "coming-out", and like all *débutantes* of high birth, she was presented to the King and Queen at Court. There followed a succession of invitations to dances, where she immediately won a string of admirers and was generally agreed to be the most accompanied dancer in London.

Of all the dashing young hopefuls it was the shy younger son of King George V who eventually captured Lady Elizabeth's heart. The Duke of York had been friends with several of the Bowes-Lyon sons for some time, but his first conscious meeting with Lady Elizabeth – apart from the legendary encounter at a children's party in 1905 when she picked the cherries off her cake and gave them to him – came in May 1920. Still known as Prince Albert then – it was a fortnight before his father made him Duke of York in that year's Birthday Honours – he was attending a dance at the London home of Lady Farquhar, and Lady Elizabeth made an impression on him which drove him to court her persistently, and to the exclusion of any other, for the next two and a half years. Another visit to Glamis followed that autumn and again in the autumn of 1921 when, according to the Duke, "Elizabeth is very kind to me. The more I see of her the more I like her." Fortunately for both of them, there were no newspaper reporters or photographers to monitor his progress and turn the whole episode into a soap opera, but the social grapevine fairly hummed with activity and the King and Queen received gratifying reports about their prospective daughter-in-law. Well briefed by Princess Mary and by Lady Airlie, the Queen's close confidante and a neighbour of the Strathmores, King George blessed his son's efforts on his first attempts to win her hand. "You'll be a lucky fellow if she accepts you," he wrote.

But the proposal was turned down. Innermost thoughts have remained private, and the reasons for Lady Elizabeth's refusal can only be intelligently speculated upon. The most plausible of them hinge upon the almost frightening leap from the easy and relatively quiet world of the landed nobility to the intransigent formality of Court life and an existence in the fierce glare of constant and sometimes highly undesirable publicity. It may have had something to do with her father's earlier, though now less justifiable, distaste for Court life, or to her own apprehension that she might neither make a good wife to a Royal Duke nor be equal to the responsibilities inescapable for anyone who became a member of his family by blood or by marriage. Lady Strathmore put it down to her being "torn between her longing to make Bertie happy and her reluctance to take on the big responsibility which this marriage must bring". In a letter penned with great sincerity to Lady Airlie, she added, "I do hope he will find a nice wife who will make him happy. I like him so much and", she concluded with her usual, almost prophetic, perception, "he is a man who will be made or marred by his wife".

Decent form dictated that, for the time being at least, that should be the end of the matter, and the Duke of York was not the sort to ignore the done thing. Being normally frustrated by setbacks, however, and unable respectably to attempt to redress his disadvantage, it is surprising that he took up his cause once again within what seems to have been a relatively short space of time. Late in 1921 the Duke, this time accompanied by his sister, paid another social visit to Glamis for one of the customary end-of-year gatherings and the following February the roles were, if anything, reversed when Lady Elizabeth came to London as one of Princess Mary's bridesmaids for her marriage to Viscount Lascelles. At the wedding breakfast at Buckingham Palace, who should the Duke of York find himself placed next to but Lady Elizabeth!

It seems that later that year, and probably as a result of the frequent references that the Duke made to Lady Elizabeth in his letters to his mother, Queen Mary and her newly-married daughter paid their respects to the Strathmores at Glamis, and towards the end of 1922 the Duke was there again, preparing the way for his next attempt at winning the lady he had wooed for two years. Early in the New Year the Strathmores came down to London and on the weekend of 12th and 13th January invited the Duke to stay at St Paul's Walden Bury. Both families knew what to expect from this visit and before leaving for Hertfordshire the Duke told his parents that he would telegraph a message to them at Sandringham as soon as he had news for them. On Sunday 13th, the Duke and Lady Elizabeth excused themselves from church – a request that seems to have been granted without the need for explanation – and went for a walk together in the woods which had once been the lady's childhood hideaway. Here the Duke made his second, and successful, proposal of marriage and soon afterwards a telegram announcing simply "Alright, Bertie" was flashed to the Norfolk countryside, to add a rare touch of magic to the repetitive royal way of life hallowed as immutable for a Sandringham January.

"We are delighted and he looks beaming!" Queen Mary enthused in her diary when, on 15th January, the Duke travelled to Sandringham to confirm his good news in person and to obtain his parents' approval. There was no mistaking his elation at the success of his enterprise and the vindication of his determined persistence. He himself admitted "I am very happy and I can only hope that Elizabeth feels the same as I do. I know I am very lucky to have won her over at last." Even the King, habitually strict with his sons and faintly suspicious of their activities and attitudes, was sufficiently moved to allow this moment of family rejoicing to mark the beginning of a slow but perceptible relaxation, at least in his relations with the Duke of York. His delighted reaction shone through his otherwise rather unimaginative and paternalistic letter of congratulation after their marriage: "You are indeed a lucky man to have such a charming and delightful wife as Elizabeth. I trust that you both will have many years of happiness before you and that you will be as happy as Mama and I am after you have been married thirty years. I can't wish you more."

Lady Elizabeth's engagement, marked by the Duke's gift to her of a platinum ring bearing a large Kashmir sapphire and two diamonds, and of a diamond naval-cap badge, was comparatively short. The Press had, rightly as it turned out, speculated for the end of April, but for some time the prospect of one of King George's rare visits abroad – to Italy – made it impossible to commit him to a date for his son's wedding. The eventual choice of Thursday 26th April left less than three months for preparations to be finalised. It was to be an occasion of considerable splendour, though the King had his own ideas about preserving the dignity of Westminster Abbey, where the ceremony was to be held, and proscribed any untoward profusion of flowers about its sanctified walls and pillars. The choice of Westminster Abbey followed recent precedent – Princess Patricia had been the only one of Queen Victoria's numerous children and grandchildren to be married there, and the Duke of York had the distinction, for the historically minded, of being the first male member of the Royal Family to marry there since Richard II married Anne of Bohemia in 1382 – and the first son of a reigning monarch to do so for over 650 years.

The Queen Mother has not always been noted for her punctiliousness but on this occasion, with a punctuality which would have done credit to Queen Mary, she emerged from the doorway of No. 17 on the arm of her father and made her way through the cheers and good wishes of the crowd to a waiting carriage. From that moment as she rode unsaluted, and escorted only by mounted policemen – she was still only a commoner – she became what the *Sunday Pictorial* called "the bridal idol", and the vision of her as she left the carriage and disappeared into the vast Abbey with its awning and red carpet, called forth the most poetic of descriptions. Her wedding dress, designed by Handley-Seymour, affected the fashionable medieval look, draped rather than fitted, ivory rather than pure white. The chiffon moire' gown was panelled across the bodice with horizontal bands of silver lame' ornamented in seed-pearl embroidery, and from waist to hem by a wide vertical band of silver and pearls threaded with ribbon. The short train that fell from her waist was made of tulle over lame' with Nottingham lace – a gesture against the import of foreign lace which at that time was contributing to swingeing unemployment in the Nottingham lace-making industry – and the tulle veil which floated over her otherwise unadorned head was edged with a length of rare Point de Flandres lace lent by Queen Mary, and secured by a chaplet of leaves. Lady Elizabeth's arms were virtually bare, covered by only the shortest of sleeves, and light satin shoes peeped from beneath the hem of the skirt. In her hands she held a bouquet of white roses, the symbol of the House of York, white heather and a sprig of myrtle taken, as royal tradition dictated, from a bush at Osborne House which Queen Victoria grew from a similar sprig in her own wedding bouquet. And as, to the sound of Elgar's Bridal March, Lady Elizabeth began her journey up the aisle, she stopped to place her flowers on the tomb of the Unknown Warrior: the myrtle, which was later removed and preserved, became the parent of two fine bushes now flourishing at Royal Lodge, the Queen Mother's Windsor home for over half a century.

It must have been an awesome sight for the bride as she neared her future husband, smartly uniformed as a Group-Captain in the RAF, complete with the resplendent Orders of the Garter and Thistle, the Garter Sash, lanyards and a string of medals. The whole eminence of the Royal Family awaited – the King resplendent in his scarlet Field-Marshal's uniform, the Queen in silver, the gaunt Queen Alexandra cloaked in ermine, a host of young and elderly princes and princesses, representatives of those branches of Queen Victoria's family who occupied royal establishments in Scandinavia, the Low Countries and the Balkans, and five Indian Princes. The Duke of York, with his groomsman the Prince of Wales in Welsh Guard's uniform, gave his bride the merest, almost furtive, glimpse and the briefest smile as she arrived and, ensconced in solemnity, they scarcely looked at each other during the ceremony. Behind her stood eight bridesmaids in green and white, with white flowers in their hair, and beyond them the congregation of almost three thousand. Before her stood the Archbishop of Canterbury, Randall Davidson, who solemnised the marriage, conducting the service which included a slight amendment to the Form prescribed by the 1662 Prayer Book, without, of course, calling into question the bride's vow to obey. The ring of yellow gold was fashioned from a nugget mined at Barmouth in mid-Wales for the purpose; the remainder of the nugget was used for the wedding rings of the bride's daughters in 1947 and 1960, her granddaughter Princess Anne in 1973 and ultimately for Diana Princess of Wales in 1981. The address was given by the then Archbishop of York, Cosmo Lang, who was to play a more dramatic role in Lady Elizabeth's life thirteen years later. Almost ominously he warned her that "You cannot resolve that your wedded life shall be happy, but you can and will resolve that it shall be noble ... The warm and generous heart of the people takes you today to itself," he continued. "Will you not in response take that heart, with all its joys and sorrows, into your own?" The register awaited the cluster of royal signatures usual on the rare occasions of this magnitude; "Elizabeth Bowes-Lyon" was modestly entered for the last time beneath the solid, plain signature of "Albert". Over a dozen British and European royalties signed, and witnesses, from the Dowager Empress of All the Russias to the Marquess of Cambridge, together with seven members of the Bowes-Lyon family, several clerics and the Prime Minister, Mr Bonar-Law, added their testimony.

The day's weather had been far from ideal and the crowds who had gathered for so many hours bore the brunt of some fierce and prolonged April showers. At some point during the morning's proceedings the rain stopped and the sun appeared, satisfying the widespread hope and belief that the bride would be blessed for ever by this overt sign of divine favour. There are, however, conflicting accounts of the transformation: some observers said that the sun came out as the bride entered the Abbey, others that she returned to Buckingham Palace in a "flood of sunlight". Yet another, more romantic, interpretation was placed upon one reporter's staunch conviction that the sun first came streaming through the Abbey windows just as Archbishop Lang's address came to its conclusion, with the words "Good luck in the name of the Lord". The King, whose memory always seemed to be faultless and who noted events with much detail, wrote in his diary that "it stopped raining at 9.30 and the sun actually came out as the Bride entered the Abbey."

To many wishful thinkers the marriage of the Duke of York and his demure and gentle bride sparked off a feeling of optimism in a discouraged world, and in those days they weren't afraid to say so. One fulsome, but by no means uniquely idyllic editorial averred that it "has made us more cheerful. We have done with the long winter, spring is in the air, all Nature is astir and May Day is at hand. The outlook, both national and international, is not so bad as it seemed three months ago. *We know we are going to pull through.*" More to the point, the marriage transformed the Duke of York's whole life every bit as much as it did for the new Duchess.

The marriage itself gave the Duke a new status in which he quietly revelled, and continued to revel for the ensuing twenty nine years. The Duchess brought him a contentment which had eluded him for a quarter of a century and he rarely felt better then when he was in her company. Official engagements at home assumed a lightness and a glow of success and high spirits of which they had until then been conspicuously bereft. Tours abroad became almost glamorous as crowds flocked to see this much-praised new member of the Royal Family, and when the Duchess became ill with tonsilitis during the 1927 visit to Australasia, the Duke wondered whether it would be better to cancel that part of the tour as he was sure that only through her could it be made a success. Eventually, of course, she gave him a family – a pair of fine daughters whose attractiveness and delightfully childish antics brought their father to a peak of popularity during the last years of the old King's reign, and the era of the growing York family has long been a byword for matrimonial contentment and vicarious popular pleasure. A long and strictly-observed period of mourning for her dead father-in-law gave the Duchess of York little opportunity to consider, far less play herself into, her new circumstances before the enervating events of 1936 began to overwhelm her. The first four weeks were effectively written off as she struggled to throw off the persistent and debilitating effects of the severe bout of influenza which had kept her away from Sandringham during the King's last illness, and when she recovered it was to find things eerily different. Just as in 1901 the then Duchess of York, later Queen Mary, had deplored the prospect of "England without the Queen (Victoria)" so the loss of another well-loved sovereign in 1936 seemed to cause the present Duchess a strange and unexplained feeling of unease. "Everything is different," she wrote in March 1936 to Lord Dawson of Penn, "especially spiritually and mentally ... I mind things that I don't like, more than before." This statement has never been authoritatively expanded upon but it has become almost renowned for its prophetic content, in view of the turmoils which the immediate future held.

There can be little doubt that the name of Wallis Simpson was too often mentioned in London Society for it to be unknown to members of the Royal Family, nor that the lady's ready fame owed everything to her popularity with the new King. As Prince of Wales, he had met her at a country house in Leicestershire five years before

crowned consort to a King pledged to defend a faith which abhorred and shunned divorce. It is unlikely that the Duchess of York envisaged anything remotely approaching her brother-in-law's abdication when, in the Spring of 1936, she and the Duke visited him, at Fort Belvedere – the visit would otherwise almost certainly not

have taken place particularly as one of the King's guests at the time was Mrs Simpson herself. This is the first recorded encounter between the two future sisters-in-law and there was suspicion from the start: Mrs Simpson noticed, with her usual ready perception, that the Duchess "was not sold" on the King's "American interest." The

hour-long meeting was not followed up until early that July when the new King gave a dinner party at York House, St. James's Palace, where both Mrs Simpson and the Yorks were amongst the guests. Again, what contact occurred was cool and it is generally reckoned to be consequent upon this event that mutual dislike between the two

and, following his usual penchant for married women, had formed a barely concealed but, in the quaint and rather hypocritical circumstances in which high society then functioned, respectable liaison. There is evidence that King George V knew of it and feared the inevitable development into a prospect of marriage and its potential for creating trouble, and both he and his heir harboured independent intentions to discuss the matter together. For various reasons, eminently understandable in the light of their uncertain and almost distrustful relationship, the problem remained unspoken of until, months after the parent's demise, it began to surface beyond further concealment. By October 1936, all those most closely concerned were in no doubt that the King wished to marry his constant companion and that, it was constitutionally impossible for her, twice divorced – as by the end of that month she was – and with both husbands living, to be

The Queen Mother, like her two daughters, always enjoys an evening out at the opera, ballet or theatre. Her stylish clothes and glittering jewellery seem to outshine all others (facing page) while her warm and bubbling personality makes any occasion seem special. Her interest in the performing arts goes far beyond that dictated by her position and she is a frequent and much-loved member of the audience at such events. Racing has always been another interest of the Queen Mother and her daughters (this page).

ladies germinated. Matters were not improved by the knowledge that Mrs Simpson was acting as hostess during the King's stay at Balmoral where he busied himself entertaining society friends on a grand scale – this to the consternation of Queen Mary, who was much put out by the conspicuous absence, for want of royal invitation, of the usual Establishment figures – nor by several other examples of the King's waywardness, the most famous being the cancellation of an official engagement in Aberdeen, ostensibly on grounds of

mourning, but in reality affording the opportunity for him to greet Mrs Simpson personally after her long train journey to Balmoral.

By all accounts, and understandably, it was a time of profound shock. With Queen Mary still grieving in early widowhood and dependent upon the support of her only daughter the Princess Royal, and with the Duke of York shattered under the mounting pressure of an inexorable destiny, it fell to the Duchess to lead the prolonged and, in events, hopeless attack against the King. The play *Crown Matrimonial* which enjoyed a lengthy success on the stage and television in the mid 1970s cast the Duchess as the

dominant adversary to King Edward, berating him for his lack of judgement, the inept handling of the issue and, above all, for keeping all his family so totally uninformed. That last score at least is well supported by evidence. Like her husband, the Duchess of York was angered at the seemingly systematic way in which the King avoided all attempts to be contacted by his brother until most of the vital decisions had effectively been made. The Duke of York finally forced a meeting, but not before the Duchess, blazing with

The Badminton Horse Trials have a magnetic attraction for the Queen Mother, who attends every April, usually with a large representation from her family. These pictures, taken in 1972, 1973 and 1977 show her with her two daughters and all six grandchildren, except for Princess Anne, a regular competitor when not prevented by the demands of motherhood.

The Order of the Garter, established by King Edward III in the fourteenth century, is the Sovereign's personal gift, and as England's most ancient and prestigious honour, it is not surprising that members of the Sovereign's family are periodically admitted to the Order. The Queen Mother, made a Lady of the Garter on King George VI's 41st birthday, and only three days after his accession, enjoys the annual June ceremony at Windsor both for its colourful traditions and for its reaffirmation of the respect in which members of her family hold this unique gift of the sovereign.

frustration, had complained, "Everyone knows more than we do. We know nothing! Nothing!"

By the early afternoon of 11th December 1936 everything *had* happened. Parliament gave effect to the Abdication Act, and in giving the Royal Assent to it, King Edward VIII ceased to be an Empire's sovereign. He was even then preparing his final broadcast to the nation before leaving for France. In his place, by automatic succession, the Duke of York assumed the throne and his Duchess, now

Queen, entered the Litany of the Church of England for the first time. Perversely she was laid low with influenza at 145 Piccadilly, ending the year much as she had started it, and she was unable to be present as the Royal Family bid tearful, incredulous farewells to the departing ex-King at Windsor. Instead, she sent him a

letter, which he read in the car which took him to Portsmouth Dockyard. Despite the past weeks' bitterness, its contents were probably devoid of unfair reproach: the character of the writer suggests the possibility; the kindly message "Hope Elizabeth better" in the exile's first telegram from France the

following morning seems to clinch it.

Whatever the King's feelings on the subject, and the evidence points to a bitter regret at the inextricable twists of successive events, the Queen's resolve remained constant and far-sighted. From the beginning of their reign she fully realised the

paramount importance of seeing her reluctant but dutiful husband established not just constitutionally but also in hearts and minds as the rightful King, and she looked forward with great single-mindedness to the immediate future, echoing Queen Mary's insistence that he needed sympathy and support. She was livid when, shortly after the Duke of Windsor's marriage in June 1937 someone reported to her that the Duchess had done wonders for him and commented that he had stopped drinking and had no unsightly pouches beneath his eyes. "Yes," she replied: "Who has the lines under his eyes now?" Indeed she found it difficult to forget that all

the strains, both mental and physical imposed upon her husband had been caused by what Queen Mary persisted in describing as King Edward's "dereliction of duty." If she resented the possibility of her husband being upstaged by his predecessor, she was adamant where the Duchess of Windsor was concerned. Conscious of the fury of Queen Mary and the other Royal ladies she felt secure in adopting an uncompromising stance in refusing to receive her, and indeed grudging the remotest acknowledgement of her. In pursuit of this rigid attitude, comprehensible perhaps only in yesterday's context, she was prepared to withstand the reported abuses heaped upon her by both the Duke and the Duchess of Windsor. Queen Mary's pivotal role was allegedly mocked by the Duchess who described the reign of George VI as a "split-

level matriarchy in pants. Queen Mary runs the King's wife and the wife runs the King." Chips Channon plaintively noted in 1937 that "certainly she (Queen Mary) and the Court hate Wallis Simpson to the point of hysteria . . . They would be better advised to be civil if it is beyond their courage to be cordial." But by and large it never happened. The Gloucesters and the Mountbattens kept in

occasional touch, and Queen Mary once sent "a kind message to your wife" in a letter to her "poor, silly son." But at the end of the Second World War, the Duke came to Windsor alone, as he did for the funerals of King George in 1952 and Queen Mary in 1953. Several private visits passed unnoticed, and recognition for the Duchess remained wanting when the family gathered again for the

The Queen Mother wearing bright blue at a flower show in 1976 (below and below left). She wore a light blue and white outfit for a service in St Paul's in 1977 (below right) and a similar flower-patterned dress, coat and hat for her 78th birthday a year later. Almost exactly a year after that she was installed as Lord Warden of the Cinque Ports at Dover and in spite of bleak August weather, she was in high spirits as (opposite page, top right) she shook hands with a long line of local dignitaries. A persistent on-shore breeze made much of that very personal, almost stylised, penchant for luxuriant feathery hats which has become almost legendary (opposite page, bottom left). Two more variations on the blue theme were seen in April 1980 when (right) she visited a convalescent home in Leatherhead and attended the thanksgiving service at the City Temple London for the 80th anniversary of the National Free Church Women's Council (far right and opposite page, top left).

funeral of the Princess Royal in 1965, and again the following year when the Duke came to London for an eye operation. When, in June 1967, a fortnight after the centenary of her birth, a plaque to the memory of Queen Mary was unveiled in the wall of Marlborough House, the

Duchess was at last seen in the ranks of the Royal Family, exchanging a few quick words with her sister-in-law the Queen Mother, though not curtseying to her as she did to the Queen. That was the only public encounter between the two old adversaries until the Duke's own

funeral in June 1972 when the Duchess, under intolerable stress and heavily sedated, may just have been conscious of the clasp of hands and the Queen Mother's murmured condolences.

After the news of the Abdication broke, the date of

the Coronation as fixed by King Edward VIII – 12th May 1937 – was not altered by his successor, the new Queen was inescapably and fully involved for five hectic months in plans for this supreme event. Basic plans were already well advanced of course, but revised procedures to accommodate the crowning of the consort as well as the King, provision for her attendants, allowances for new invitees, and for original invitees who might

*The Queen Mother wearing two of
her favourite tiaras in recent years.
(Right) arriving at the London
Palladium in November 1980 for the
Royal Variety Performance, where
she met the infamous "J.R." (below),
Sammy Davis Jnr., and Arthur
Askey (bottom) among many others.
(Far right) being welcomed by the
Prime Minister, Margaret Thatcher,
for dinner at No. 10 Downing Street
the same month. More evenings out
(opposite page): a reception at the
Japanese Embassy (bottom left)
during Emperor Hirohito's visit in
1971; a visit to the Royal Opera
House to see* Mayerling *in Febuary
1978 (top left); meeting the stars at
the Royal Film Performance in
March 1981 (right).*

no longer wish to attend, progressively complex planning committee considerations, and host of minor and more personal decisions had now to be embraced. As on previous royal occasions, these included the knotty question of the role of the broadcasting media which again became the subject of hot and formidable debate. Ultimately it was agreed that a further innovation should be permitted – that of having the Coronation service filmed and broadcast live, but with television cameras (then a complete novelty) restricted to outside coverage only. At the other end of the decision-making process the Queen

decided to wear the famous Koh-I-Noor diamond as the principal jewel in her crown. The diamond, which was presented to Queen Victoria in 1850 is thought to bring ill-luck on any man who wears it, but Queen Elizabeth was content to rely on its history as the bringer of good fortune to its female wearers. The dictates of superstition may well have been made more easy by what many contemporary observers saw as the patent and solemn attitude of faith with which both the King and Queen approached their Coronation. In today's sceptical world it is almost fashionable to wonder about the sincerity of any public

significance of the forthcoming Coronation while the Queen, already a good friend of the Archbishop of Canterbury, wrote soon after the Abdication a letter of genuine appreciation to him which she signed "Yours for the first time and with great affection, Elizabeth R." In it she revealed with quiet satisfaction that "I can hardly now believe that we have been called to this tremendous task and the curious thing is that we are not afraid. I feel that God has enabled us to face the situation calmly." Now, not long after an incident in which she is reputed to have lost her nerve and cried out, "I can't go through with it! I can't be

There was a reduced royal contingent at the Badminton Horse Trials in April 1982, with the Queen and Prince Philip in Canada, the Prince and Princess of Wales preparing for their Scillies holiday, and Prince Andrew sailing towards the South Atlantic with the Falkland's Task Force. But the Queen Mother was there as usual, escorted by the Duke of Beaufort (above).

act of worship in the course of a function of State, but in 1937, far from emulating the sort of public behaviour which had caused Bishop Blunt of Bradford to speak out so uncompromisingly against Edward VIII, the King and Queen made no secret of their religious faith. The Bishop of St Alban's felt able to write to the Queen pointing out the religious

crowned!" she and her husband met the Archbishop on the Sunday before the Coronation for a discussion about the spiritual meaning of the rite. "I gave them my personal blessing," noted the Archbishop afterwards. "There were tears in their eyes when we rose from our knees. From that moment I knew what would be in their hearts when they came to their anointing and crowning." The Poet Laureate, John Masefield echoed the sentiment in his "Prayer for the King's Reign":– "Grant to our Queen the strength that lifts and shares The daily burden that a monarch bears," and some weeks after the Coronation Harold Nicolson observed from the attitude and behaviour of the King and Queen that there was "no doubt they had entered on this task with a real religious sense." The Coronation festivities began well enough – from the sumptuous State Banquet for 450 people in the Ball and

mistakes and near misses, all of which were duly noted by the King, who later confessed to Ramsay MacDonald that for long periods during the ceremony he was unaware of what he was doing. Unusually for her, Queen Mary, whose sense of occasion led her to break with the tradition whereby the widow of a previous sovereign did not attend the Coronation of any successor, was unaware of any mistakes. "Bertie and Elizabeth looked so well when they came in and did it all beautifully," she recorded, thrilled on the verge of her seventieth birthday to have

witnessed the crowning of the first consort since the sixteenth century to come of British stock. The irrepressible Chips Channon soaked up the scene as that Consort entered the Abbey wearing her dress of ivory satin and a magnificent purple velvet robe and train, embroidered with the emblems of the principal Dominions of the Empire and carried by six trainbearers. "She appeared dignified but smiling," he commented, adding – with a touch of mischief perhaps triggered off by persistent rumours that the Queen was pregnant – "and much more

Supper Room at Buckingham Palace to the moving personal interludes in which the King complimented his wife's indispensable support by offering her the South African-jewelled insignia of the Thistle – thus making her the first ever Lady of that great Scottish Order – and in which Queen Mary presented her daughter-in-law with a tortoiseshell and diamond fan which had once belonged to Queen Alexandra. The King received from her a dark blue enamel snuffbox bearing miniatures of his parents. But Coronation Day itself – like the Wedding Day in 1923 – proved to be dull and showery and the Queen's procession to Westminster Abbey was halted when a chaplain fainted *en route* and could not conveniently be removed to receive first aid. The ceremony itself was full of

bosomy." Princesses Elizabeth and Margaret attended as well; supervised by Queen Mary they witnessed the solemn and unforgettable moment of their mother's consecration as the Archbishop blessed her, anointed her as she sat concealed beneath a canopy of cloth of gold held by four duchesses, and finally placed the consort's crown, set into Queen Victoria's circlet, upon her head. Who would have noticed the irony as, following this sacred procedure, the King's right-hand

The Queen Mother has attended all the major weddings which now form part of our Royal Family's recent history. Attendants perpetuate the family connections: Princess Anne was bridesmaid to Princess Margaret in May 1960 (right); Lady Sarah Armstrong-Jones attended both Princess Anne in November 1973 (bottom right) and the Princess of Wales in July 1981 (below). Periodic gatherings of the royal clan (opposite page) allow the gradual changes to be marked for posterity.

woman took her place on his left-hand side?

Throughout her time as consort, and indeed as Duchess, the Queen Mother was a noted leader of fashion, just as her grandson's wife is today. It was she who popularised the cloche hats of the 1920s, but in the 1930s the fashionable requirement changed considerably. The close-fitting hats gave way to large, fanciful picture hats with enormous brims. Long, floaty dresses superseded the short, straight skirts of the previous decade, and parasols, with which Queen Mary herself had never dispensed, came back into fashion. The new luxuriant look reached its peak in the years immediately before the Second World War, when Norman Hartnell, one of whose earliest royal assignments had been to

design a wedding dress for the Duchess of Gloucester in 1935, was snapped up by the Duchess of York. When she became Queen he effectively became Couturier Royal, and no royal patronage could have been better timed. His first years in his enviable new station coincided with the pre-war heyday of European fashion houses, and the Queen was the willing beneficiary of all their influence on his efforts to lend flair to the current expression of royalty as a social and diplomatic force.

That attitude was particularly relevant for the State Visit to

France, which the King and Queen undertook as the first of their reign in 1938. The visit had been scheduled to begin on 28th June, the one hundredth anniversary of Queen Victoria's Coronation, but the death, five days before, of the Countess of Strathmore threw the arrangements into confusion. The Queen, saddened at this unfortunate coincidence as much by the loss of a dearly-loved mother, went immediately into deep mourning, and the journey to France was subsequently postponed until 19th July. It was almost delayed again by the King's severe attack

of gastric influenza, but that passed in time for the visit to begin as freshly arranged. The Queen left Britain still dressed in black, but her arrival in France could not have been more surprising. Using the widespread European practice of wearing white for mourning as a convenient excuse, she stepped onto French soil, confident and smiling in brilliant white, and the entire three-day visit was carried out in the same elegant vein. Extravagantly sweeping Edwardian-style gowns predominated, along with crinolines said to have been inspired by Winterhalter's

Prominent as ever on the Royal Family's big day out at Epsom, the Queen Mother takes her usual expert interest in the Derby, along with the Queen (right), Prince Philip (far right), Princess Anne (above), the Duke of Gloucester (centre left), Princess Michael of Kent (opposite page, top left) and the Ogilvys (above right). Although the Queen Mother runs horses only in National Hunt races, she shares the Queen's enthusiasm for the Flat.

(Overleaf) the Royal Family at Ascot.

famous portraits of the young Queen Victoria, all complementing the fine, favourable summer weather and the theatrical outdoor performances of song and dance which the French put on for their royal guests. The Queen's graceful, airy wardrobe was perfectly shown off by her slow, dignified gait – what Chips Channon later called "her curious sideways lilting walk" – and balanced by her sizeable collection of huge, frilled, wide-brimmed hats and delicate white lace parasols. The French, impressed as much by this vision as by her competent, easy

command of their language, were immediately won over. "Today France is a monarchy again," trumpeted the Parisian press. "We have taken the Queen to our hearts. She rules over two nations."

The visit was of course a declaration of solidarity in the face of what many people saw as a coming conflict with Germany, and the following months were heavy with diplomatic activity all over Western Europe, devoted to staving off what ultimately proved unstoppable. Much of Mr Chamberlain's business as Prime Minister necessitated the King's continued presence in London, and he was unable to be present for the grand launching of the liner *Queen Elizabeth* at the end of September 1938. The Queen

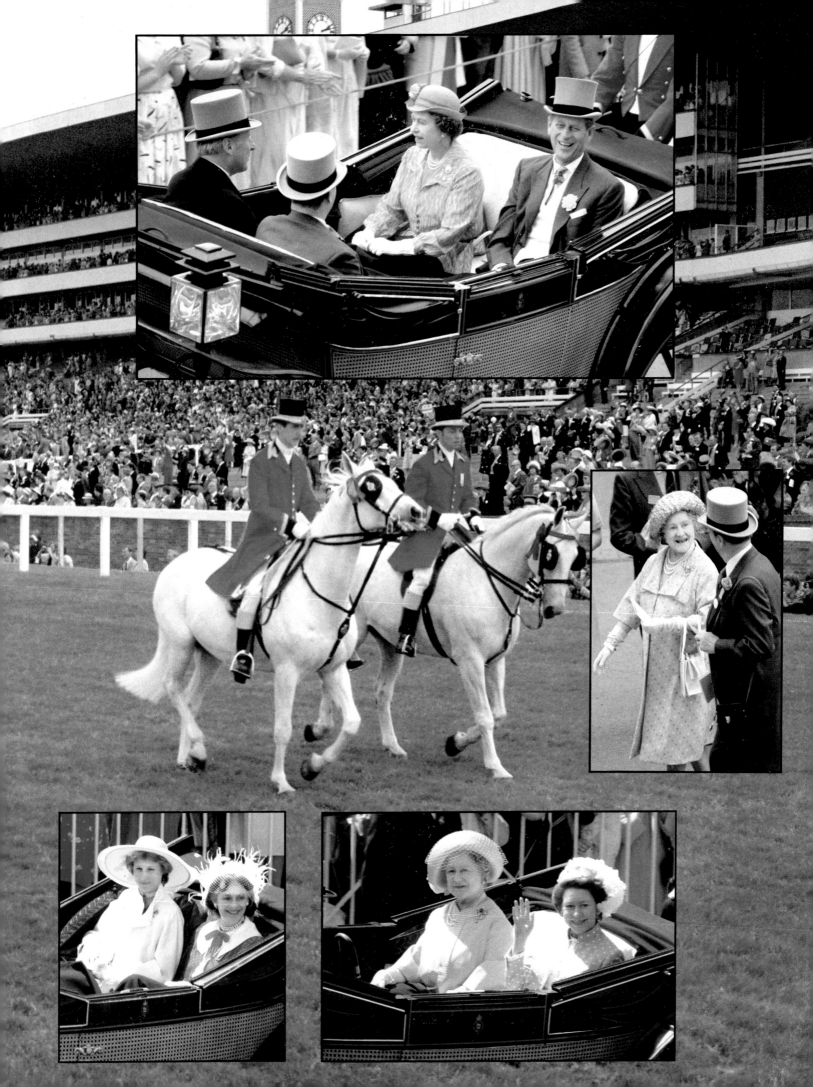

The Queen Mother and relatives at Badminton, April 1982. Youngest grandson Prince Edward escorted her to Badminton church on the final day (below) while the Duchess of Beaufort emerged with the Queen Mother after the service (right).

travelled to Clydeside alone, passing on her husband's words of comfort in phrases now famous for their rather quaint, old fashioned optimism: "I have a message for you from the King. He bids the people of this country to be of good cheer ..." But cheer was hard to come by in those lowering days of continued political crises. Even when, in May 1939, the King and Queen sailed to the New World, they had to forego the originally planned use of the battleship *Repulse,* in case it was

(Overleaf) *special cheers greeted the Queen Mother at the wedding of the Prince and Princess of Wales at St Paul's Cathedral in 1981. Escorted by Prince Edward to the service, and by Prince Andrew for the return journey, she looked thrilled with the splendour and pageantry of it all. As the bride and groom walked down the aisle, a broad beam of delight lit up her face, though she had dabbed away the occasional tear during the more solemn moments of the marriage service.*

required at short notice for war service: they travelled in the liner *Empress of Australia* instead. For the Queen in particular, the trip was greatly exciting, and the adrenalin certainly flowed when she found that the ship was surrounded by icebergs off the coast of Newfoundland. "We

very nearly hit an iceberg the day before yesterday," she wrote to Queen Mary, "and the poor Captain was nearly demented because some kind cheerful people kept reminding him that it was about here that the *Titanic* was struck and just about the same date."

When war finally came, at 11 o'clock on Sunday 3rd September, the Queen was still at Balmoral with the two Princesses. She came down South to join the King immediately, leaving her daughters to complete as much as possible of what would be

their last proper summer holiday at Queen Victoria's famous Highland retreat. For Balmoral became one of the Royal Family's war casualties, being closed down for the six-year duration of hostilities. Sandringham was another victim: shortly after Christmas

1939 the Big House was closed
and its lawns and golf course
ploughed up for food
production, though in 1943 the
King and his family would spend
a short harvest-time holiday on
the estate. Windsor Castle was a
sorry sight compared with its
peacetime glories – all pictures
and hangings were removed and
boxed, furniture was put into
safe storage and its many
resounding corridors were only

*Royal Ascot is another of the Queen
Mother's annual magnets, and while
she is no fashion extrovert, she enjoys
the opportunity to wear some of her
colourful summery outfits. The daily
order of royal processions changes as
different members of her family join
the festival: (this page) with the
Queen in 1982; (opposite page) with
the Queen and Lady Diana Spencer
in 1981, and with Princess
Margaret in 1982.*

from the Royal estates, for instance, and it is unlikely that the special regulations governing food rations for official purposes were not extended to the Royal Family. But there can be no doubt that the King and Queen in particular shared the dangers common to their subjects in London and indeed all of Britain's major cities and industrial centres. It is almost certain that plans were well laid to whisk them away to safety in the event of a German invasion – an organisation called the Coates mission had in fact been established to remove them to one of four country houses – and arrangements for an eventual escape to Canada to head a Government in exile have been profusely rumoured.
But while Britain remained uninvaded, the Queen voiced

dimly lit by single electric lights. And Buckingham Palace itself, grand and solid as it was, did not escape the immediate effect of the austerities of war. Even its most august wartime guest, Mrs Eleanor Roosevelt, had to suffer them: the Queen offered the use of her own bedroom which the President's wife was astounded to find both cold and damp – "just one little bar of electric fire in the room" – while the daily quota of bathwater was limited to a few inches, and the grandiose royal crockery bore very ordinary canteen food. The exact degree of royal privations during the war has never been authoritatively documented. There were occasional supplies of game

both her preference for remaining in London and her conception of duty to do so. These emerged during a conversation with Harold Nicolson in July 1940, when he shamefacedly confessed having them in a message broadcast on Armistice Day, 1939 – she kept her own children with her in London. When, however, the Blitz began in earnest some ten months later, Princesses Elizabeth and Margaret were

felt homesick whilst abroad recently. "But that is all right," answered the Queen. "That's personal patriotism. I should die if I had to leave." Her sense of duty in particular was explained in an oft-quoted chain of irrefutable logic on the question of the evacuation of her two daughters, in which she is reputed to have said, "They cannot go without me. I cannot go without the King. The King will never leave." That, in fact, left her open to criticism in that while she was encouraging the mothers of London to allow their children to be evacuated to unknown destinations – "We know what it means to be parted from our children," she assured

sent to Windsor to continue their studies while London braced itself for the fury of Hitler's all-night bombing. From the German point of view the bombardment of September 1940 was disappointing and unsuccessful but it sent the Londoners, for whom this was the first real taste of modern

The wedding of Mr Nicholas Soames, grandson of Sir Winston Churchill, to Miss Catherine Weatherall provided another opportunity for a family outing. The Queen Mother took Princess Margaret, the Prince of Wales and Lady Diana Spencer to the service, held at St Margaret's Church Westminster in May 1981.

warfare, reeling. Vast areas of the closely packed East End were destroyed and hundreds of civilian lives were lost as makeshift air-raid shelters proved ineffective against the might of the Luftwaffe in full cry. Both the King and Queen – the Queen was later to describe the Cockney as "a great fighter" – paid immediate and almost unscheduled visits to the devastated suburbs, unable to do more than comfort the bereaved, show concern for the homeless and encourage those

working to mitigate suffering. These visits became almost daily events as the constant and intense German attack bit deeper into London's morale – so deep, in fact, that the Royal couple were actually booed on one East End visit in mid-September. This hostility was a manifestation of what many politicians already feared – the breaking of the country's spirit in the face of hopeless odds – and even Clement Davies considered that by continuing to hammer away at the densely populated and deprived East End the Führer could effectively have occasioned anarchy in Britain and solved many of his own problems into the bargain. But Hitler made the mistake of

face."
If life thus became somewhat more comfortable psychologically, its physical comforts fast began to disappear. Although the only part of the Palace to receive a direct hit during a total of nine raids on it was the chapel – bombed during Morning Service with the loss of a hundred lives and of almost every chattel save the massive Royal Family Bible – extensive areas of the grounds and courtyards were hit, and much of the Palace's structure was reduced to so much rubble by the impact. The main drainage system was blown and the Queen particularly remembered that "a great column of water came into the air" as a bomb was dropped

spreading the bombardment to London's West End, thus subjecting the wealthy to dangers and deprivations similar to the capital's poorer citizens. Not unexpectedly, Buckingham Palace itself came in for several air attacks and it may have been with some relief that the Queen was consequently able to say, after the most severe damage had been done, "I'm glad we've been bombed. It makes me feel I can look the East End in the

from a plane which had flown straight up the Mall and over the Palace. She also remembered that the resulting flooding brought the rats out into the garden, and that "everyone had great fun pursuing them." Holes gaped in roofs and ceilings – the Queen's own apartments were damaged when a bomb dropped straight through them, without

The Queen Mother paid a visit to Canada House in London to open its new cultural centre in February 1982. This official engagement would have brought back personal memories: it was her last before the thirtieth anniversary of the death of her husband, with whom she carried out a successful, extremely popular, six week visit to Canada in 1939.

exploding, into the ground floor rooms below – and an ingenious network of baths and buckets cluttered many passages and corridors when the rain came through. A new swimming pool, built for the family only two years earlier, was cratered out of

all recognition and before long no window remained intact throughout the entire building of six hundred rooms. Quite apart from the damage wrought by successive explosions, the King and Queen were unnerved by the risks of unexploded bombs,

one of which is even today thought to be embedded deep down "somewhere in the garden, I suppose," and by the fact that "one really wasn't quite sure what was going to disappear next."

They nevertheless decided that, in the Queen's words "we stay put with our people" and, despite the repeated strain of seeing, not only at first hand but also at first opportunity, when things were at their most harrowing, the daily toll in life, limb, property and morale which the war exacted, continued their seemingly unending programme of hastily-arranged, ill-prepared but utterly spontaneous visits. When they were not surveying the ruins of Coventry, Hull, Portsmouth, Bath or Manchester they were inspecting the British war effort in every department, from ammunition

factories to first aid posts and from defence command centres to local air raid shelters. Usually the King wore the uniform of one or other of the armed services, while the Queen dressed plainly, but impeccably, a combination which befitted the austerity-ridden circumstances as well as the morale-raising objectives of her missions. Nowhere were they any longer remotely unpopular: everywhere, vast crowds emerged from side streets and the wreckage of decent homes to reciprocate the royal gesture, and it was on occasions like those that the Queen initiated

what we now take for granted as the walkabout. Harold Nicolson spotted it during their visit to Sheffield in January 1941: "When the car stops, the Queen nips out into the snow and goes straight into the middle of the crowd and starts talking to them. For a moment or two they just gaze and gape in astonishment. But then they all start talking at once: 'Hi! Your Majesty! Look here! . . .'"

It was an agonisingly long haul from the turn of the tide in 1943 to the achievement of full European peace – and victory – in May 1945, but when it happened the "brief moment of rejoicing" was overwhelming. The Royal Family appeared on the Palace balcony whose tasselled drapes concealed the evidence of the bomb damage, against a backdrop of shattered and blacked-out casements. Prime Minister Churchill, who joined them there, was speechless with emotion at the honour of it. The King looked solemn as if inwardly grateful and relieved by the deliverance which had once seemed impossible. The Queen looked triumphant, her two daughters suddenly immensely grown-up. In the plethora of parades and processions that followed, there was none of that resentment

which had soured at least one royal visit to the East End in 1940. Just as in 1941 the Queen had, according to President Roosevelt's Personal Assistant, "found it extremely difficult to find words to express her feelings towards the people of Britain – she thought their actions magnificent and that victory in the long run was sure," so now a celebrating Irishwoman in London's Commercial Road reciprocated with a blunter but equally articulate tribute: "I always was partial to royalty – and still am!"

The British Royal House, like most of the constitutional

monarchies of Europe with the exception of Belgium, came through the War and its whirlwind aftermath dominated by the Soviet push from the East, not only unscathed but strengthened. It must have been with utter dismay that the King and Queen saw their distant relatives and fellow monarchs liquidated or bundled out of their eastern European lands as Roumania, Bulgaria and Yugoslavia fell to Communist republicanism just as in 1918 Austria, Prussia and Russia had collapsed under the weight of humiliating defeats at the hands of their adversaries. In Greece the monarchy, which had never in the previous quarter century been sufficiently stable to increase its chances of survival, swayed this way and that at the mercy of politicians of the left and right, and the Italians wasted little time ridding themselves of King Victor

Emmanuel III and his son of short reign, Umberto II. But as the remaining western European monarchs returned from exile to their homelands, the British Royal Family were able to command the spontaneous affection and loyalty of the surging masses who surrounded Buckingham Palace, for having been with them throughout the worst bombing and the privations of this most cataclysmic of wars. The Queen even received a poem from a lady in Chicago, praising her for "wearing your gayest gown, your bravest smile . . . when London Bridge was

great tribute on the many occasions when the victory was celebrated. In nine of the most challenging years, particularly for sovereigns of such little previous first-hand experience, they had triumphed – and all by their own efforts.

It was all the more unfair, therefore, that when the opportunity came, as it now did, for consolidation and the luxury of looking back with some satisfaction on what had gone before, the King and Queen – particularly the Queen on whom the burden eventually fell – should have had such a hard time of it. The horror of war

burning down," and Eleanor Roosevelt, ever the most dispassionate of commentators, averred that "in all my contacts with them I have gained the greatest respect for the King and Queen. Both of them are doing an extraordinarily outstanding job for the people. You admire their character and devotion to duty." Little wonder therefore, that the King and Queen found themselves the objects of such

Britain and the Commonwealth paid enthusiastic tributes to the Queen Mother amid celebrations to mark her 80th birthday. On 15th July 1980, some three weeks in advance, London was the scene of colourful processions as the Royal Family, including Princess Alice and the Duchess of Gloucester (far left), Princess Anne, Princess Margaret, Lady Sarah Armstrong-Jones (above left), and the Queen, Prince Philip and Prince Edward (above) attended a thanksgiving service in St Paul's Cathedral. The Archbishop of Canterbury delivered a moving and appreciative address ending with the words "Thank you, Your Majesty. Thanks be to God". Crowds swarmed round Buckingham Palace to acclaim the Queen Mother when she appeared on its balcony afterwards.

gave way to an uneasy peace, and one which at home brought the long trial of austerity as the new Labour Government wrestled to reconcile their sincerely-held Socialist principles with the need to put the economy back on its feet. This was not helped by the appalling winter of 1946/47 when shortages of food and fuel were aggravated by months of freezing weather and almost insurmountable transport difficulties. The embarrassment thus felt by the King and Queen,

speeches during that tour, and the Queen confirmed his unease: "it is doubly hard for Bertie, who feels he should be at home," she wrote to Queen Mary. "We think of home all the time."

The visit, bursting with sunshine, celebration and song, was famous for the fact that Princess Elizabeth and Princess Margaret – then twenty and sixteen respectively – joined their parents for the first time on a major official tour. It is now particularly remembered for the

for whom a visit to South Africa had been planned many months beforehand, was acute as they realised the irony of their being in warm, sunny climes while their fellow countrymen were suffering perpetual and worsening assaults on their welfare. The King referred to his dilemma several times in his

elder daughter's dedication of her "whole life, whether it be long or short" to the service of the peoples of the Commonwealth and Empire, on her twenty-first birthday that April. Already it seemed that the King and Queen, conscious of their own sad lack of preparation for the Throne, were schooling

their daughter for the time – though little did they suspect its proximity – when she would take over the reigns of constitutional power.

Yet there was another, more subtle reason for the Princess' inclusion on the tour. She had already developed an affection for a young naval lieutenant,

Prince Philip of Greece who, like her, was a great-great-grandchild of Queen Victoria and thus her third cousin. It is still a matter of some conjecture as to when this mutual attachment was first conceived. Although the couple met during a visit which the King and Queen made to Dartmouth in

and that is why he is in our Navy." It was however more than evident to an eagle-eyed Press that the look which Prince Philip gave Princess Elizabeth while taking her fur jacket from her as she entered Westminster Abbey for the wedding of Mountbatten's daughter Patricia in 1946 proclaimed something deeper than his natural flair for impeccable, gentlemanly behaviour.

It was a good guess, and indeed it seems from later correspondence between the

Less formal, but equally loyal and sincere congratulations surrounded the Queen Mother when, on 4th August 1980, she made her annual public appearance outside Clarence House to receive tributes from the Household Brigades (left) and vocal greetings from the crowds.

1939, it seems clear, especially for the thirteen-year-old Princess, no ulterior motive existed, except possibly in the mind of Lord Louis Mountbatten, Prince Philip's uncle, who had for many years been rumoured to have pressed the claims of members of his family for the hand of successive heirs to the Throne. The Duke of Edinburgh has pooh-poohed the notion that there was some long term plan to match him with the heiress presumptive, and in particular has dismissed Chips Channon's well-aimed guess as early as 1942 that "he is to be our future Prince Consort,

King and his daughter that she had wanted a fairly early engagement. But arrangements for the South African tour were too well advanced to allow for Princess Elizabeth's withdrawal, as she would no doubt have preferred, and it appears that the Queen was instrumental in persuading her to give her feelings time to settle. Shortly after her wedding in November 1947, the Princess wrote to her mother that she fully appreciated the wisdom of waiting before becoming engaged, and another example of the Queen's tactful and wise influence as a concerned mother came to a successful conclusion. This first post-war royal wedding, though restricted by the observance of austerity measures which even for the Royal Family were still in force, provided a rare moment of colour in a grey world. Out came the gleaming royal carriages, and the bride who, we are told, had to save up her ration coupons for months in advance to obtain enough material for her wedding dress, contrasted sweetly – ensconced in its soft white – with the blaze of scarlet and black from the uniforms of the troops lining the streets of London. For the first time since the beginning of hostilities the

Vendors of balloons (bottom) and other souvenirs did a roaring trade as young and old clamoured to offer cards, flowers and gifts to Britain's most popular octogenarian. The Queen Mother's immediate family stood with her at the gates of Clarence House and the Queen and Princess Margaret lent a hand in taking the weight of their mother's unending stream of presents.

soldiers were out of khaki, and the capital saw ceremonial in full colour as it had not done for almost a decade.

For all that, these November festivities were a mere foretaste of another celebration soon to come. On 26th April 1948, the King and Queen reached their Silver Wedding anniversary, and on a bright and sunny spring Monday they rode in carriage procession to St Paul's Cathedral for a thanksgiving service. It was not just the sky that was blue: as if in tribute to the Queen's favourite colour, Princess Elizabeth wore a china blue dress with a blue fox cape, and Princess Margaret – now a rising eighteen-year-old – was dressed in a deep blue outfit. The Queen matched her daughters with a silver-blue full length gown with a sweeping train – a model of the New Look era which better times were ushering into the fashion world.

On her dress appeared the Order of the Garter and two family orders, and a large, fluffy boa was slung warmly round her neck. With her now famed, matronly smile and gracious wave, she sat beside the King, who had chosen naval uniform for the day, as through the deafening cheers of the heavily-lined streets and to the distant thunder of gun salutes and bray of trumpet fanfares they reached St Paul's where a capacity congregation took part in the

service.
Back at Buckingham Palace, 150 guests were entertained to a three-course luncheon, and a large cake bearing the coats of arms of the King and Queen was cut. That evening they toured the East End, encountering street after street blocked by

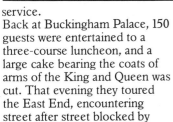

A favourite deep-tourquoise velvet outfit almost matching the Queen Mother's eyes, was seen frequently in 1982, as in February (above, top right and far left) when she visited St Peter's Church Walworth for a thanksgiving service, and the following month when she opened the Kingston YMCA at Surbiton (left and opposite page).

happiness, for the next four
years were beset by the anxieties
and upsets caused by a
repetitive and steady
deterioration in the King's
health. By the end of 1948 he
was out of action with severe
circulatory trouble and
hardening of the arteries set in.
The danger of gangrene
presented itself and at one time
it was feared that the King might
have to have a leg amputated.
The development could not
have come at a more trying time
– Princess Elizabeth was then in
the advanced stages of her first
pregnancy – but the Queen was
resigned to bearing much of the
burden of worry herself. She
gave instructions that her
daughter was not to be informed

of the full extent of her father's
condition, and during the
increasing pressure of duties that
her deputising for the King
entailed, she radiated that
outward, pleasurable calm which
the experience of previous years
had taught her to maintain, no
matter how hostile the
circumstances. It was
particularly distressing to be
deprived of Princess Elizabeth's
company the following year,
when she went to join her
husband in Malta where he was
serving with the Royal Navy.
The King responded well to
treatment and, in the cautious
optimism of the New Year,
undertook a few engagements.
By March, however, the blood-
flow to his legs was found to be

cheering crowds who swarmed
round the royal car, even
throwing flowers through the
window onto the Queen's lap.
The 21-mile drive was such a
success that they were half an
hour late returning to the
Palace, arriving only just in time
to give a pre-arranged broadcast
to the nation. The King, quietly
grateful for the day's show of
intense popular loyalty,
struggled to express his
appreciation: it was as if he now
knew how almost bewildered his
father had been at the acclaim
his people gave him at the Silver
Jubilee. The Queen joined in
the broadcast, emphasising her
concern for those still facing the
privations of post-war life: "My
heart goes out to all who are
living in uncongenial
surroundings and who are
longing for the time when they
will have a home of their own.
The world today is longing to
find the secret of community,
and all married lives are in a
sense communities in
miniature."
As it happened, the Silver
Wedding marked the end of an
all too brief period of unallayed

still obstructed, and further
treatment – a lumbar
sympathectomy – proved
necessary and for the time being
successful. He began to resume
a gentle programme of duties,
but already he was beginning to
look painfully thin, a
prematurely ageing man with
wispy, greying hair – a shadow, it
seems with hindsight, of worse
things to come. Even so, he was

able to enjoy life and at a cocktail party of the Duke of Kent's Buckinghamshire home in June 1950, he was said to be looking "much younger than the Duke of Windsor," while the Queen, stoically accepting what was and what had to be, continued to withstand the trials of those waning years. She "looked sublime," according to Chips Channon in 1951. "I really marvelled at her self-possession."

months claim her husband's life. Sharing that information with her daughters but, naturally, keeping it from the three-year-old Prince Charles, who was a frequent and welcome young guest at Buckingham Palace while his parents were absent from home on successive official duties abroad, the Queen continued to act in public as if untroubled by any doubt about the King's health. Even on that January day in 1952, when they both walked onto the tarmac at London Airport to see Princess Elizabeth and her husband off on a Commonwealth tour which the King was too ill to make himself, the Queen kept up that cheerful, almost chatty spirit which had characterised her

As we now know, she was to need all the self-possession she could muster that year. In May, soon after the King had in the presence of the entire Royal Family opened the Festival of Britain, he fell ill with influenza, and an inspection of the left lung, which had been severely affected by catarrhal inflammation, exposed a malignant growth. In an operating theatre specially set up at Buckingham Palace, he underwent a delicate operation to remove his lung by resection, and throughout that agonising treatment and the week of anxiety that followed, the Queen hardly left his side.

Gradually, the King regained his strength, but by then the Queen knew that cancer had taken its hold and would in a matter of public appearances in all the harrowing preceding months. But she knew, and the pitifully preoccupied look on the King's face made it clear that he knew too, that this would be his last sight of his daughter. It was a cold and windy day, and the King, gaunt, staring, swamped in a heavy great-coat yet bare-headed, strained for a last lingering look of the departing Argonaut aircraft. Then he made his leaden-hearted way back to Buckingham Palace, and thence eventually to Sandringham. It was there that he spent 5th February shooting hares at Flitcham, on the Sandringham Estate, while the Queen and

grief when the blow fell, his death marked not only the loss of a husband but also of a position and a way of life. The relentless and unquestioning machinery of dynastic succession which had already operated at the unwatched hour of the King's demise, took its automatic course and Princess Elizabeth was, in her absence, proclaimed Queen, succeeding her mother as first lady in the land. We are not told whether, on her arrival back at Buckingham Palace the following day, the new Queen was curtsied to by her mother, as Queen Mary did at Marlborough House that

Princess Margaret motored across Norfolk for a cruise on the Broads and a visit to the painter Edward Seago, joining the King back at the Big House that evening. And it was there too that in the small hours of the following day he died, discovered at daybreak by his valet who had brought his early morning tea.

To the Queen, whose long expectation of the inevitable could not soften the crush of

afternoon – "her old granny and subject must be the first to do her homage," – but the point does not need forcing. From then on Queen Elizabeth, adopting the title of Queen Mother as Queen Alexandra had done in 1910, took second place. Clarence House and Queen Elizabeth the Queen Mother have become almost synonymous in the last thirty years, just as Marlborough House had been with Queen

Mid-May 1982 found the Queen Mother in Paris, visiting France once again as she has, on and off, since her teens. This particular visit was part private, part official, the main official purpose being to open a new wing of the Hertford British Hospital, of which she is Patron, on 12th May – the 45th anniversary of her Coronation. That afternoon, she took tea with President Mitterrand who accompanied Her Majesty to the main entrance of the Elyse'e Palace (these pages) for her departure. Having visited France officially five times in the previous quarter of a century, and on many other private occasions, the Queen Mother knows the Bordeaux region, and the Chateaux of the Loire well. It is said that she influenced the decision to send Princess Anne for a stay in France in the early 1960s.

Mary. It is in fact part of St James's Palace, which it effectively adjoins, and has been described – in a rather vain attempt to make it sound remotely comparable to anything in the more common run of houses – as two back-to-back houses joined into one. It was built by John Nash for King William IV when he was Duke of Clarence, in 1825, almost forty years after he had first occupied a house on the same site. Queen Victoria's mother had lived there for twenty years, and it eventually became the home – though not much lived in – of Arthur, Duke of

Connaught until his death, as Queen Victoria's last surviving son, in 1942. After serving as a Red Cross headquarters for five years, it was taken over in 1949 and much modernised, as White Lodge had been in its day, by Princess Elizabeth and the Duke of Edinburgh, whose second child Princess Anne was born there in August 1950. The Queen Mother has succeeded, as no other royal occupant this century, in making it the perfect permanent London home. Although it houses administrative offices, and despite the noble display of royal insignia outside – even the

lamp-posts are surmounted by miniature crowns – its cream-painted exterior and heavy, highly-polished mahogany doors enclose a spacious, restful house which in design, furnishing and ornamentation is *very* Queen Mother. A plethora of silver trophies chart her satisfyingly successful thirty-five-year old career as a race-horse owner; glass-fronted cabinets house her collection of Red Anchor period Chelsea china, accumulated over many years; her weakness for Regency wine coasters is revealed, and the huge mirrors and chandeliers, the heavy velvet drapes and valances at the windows add luxurious style to this otherwise homely building. Her private sitting-room sports a marble mantlepiece built, before the house itself, in the mid-18th century, but the Queen Mother's taste for the more modern expressions of art are epitomised by the wide variety of pictures she has collected: Sickert, the English impressionist, she is very fond of; L.S. Lowry she discovered before most other

After her annual tour of the Cinque Ports in June 1982 the Queen Mother sailed in the Royal Yacht Britannia *to Portsmouth where she disembarked (top left) to a warm welcome from waiting crowds. A Royal Wedding glass goblet (top) provided a change from the usual bouquets.*

There was a faint hint of mischief in the Queen Mother's eye (below, far right) when in May 1982 she visited Smithfield Market and became the delighted target of good natured Lése-majesté at the hands of its many Cockney stall-holders. Interspersed among the formalities of her tour of London's most famous meat market, organised to celebrate the centenary of the first meat shipment from New Zealand to Britain, were spontaneous acts of gallantry from meat cutters, porters and packers as they seized her hands and kissed them, and serenaded her inspection of the main hall with patriotic songs.

people did; Edward Seago is well patronised by the Royal Family, and all have a place here. Alongside are such occasional paintings as a portrait of King George VI investing Princess Elizabeth with the Order of the Garter, and an uncompleted portrait of the Queen Mother herself by Augustus John: he started it during the War, but never finished it, and when he died the directors of a company who took over his premises found the portrait and presented it to her. "It has cheered me up no end," she said after she received it.

In the meantime, the Queen

There is arguably no subject nearer to the Queen Mother's heart, nor more readily identified with her than that of the garden. Her patronage of the London Gardens Society is now long established, and marked by her annual tours of prize-winning gardens in various parts of the capital. On 14th July 1982 she visited gardens in Kensington (these pages) and Wandsworth, casting an expert eye (top centre) as she wandered through allées, engaging in erudite horticultural conversation with her hosts.

Mother had busied herself with acquiring another home, and something different from anything she had lived in before. It says a great deal for her vigour and search for new life amid the desolation of widowhood that she was in the mood to spot a good prospect when it presented itself, and it was during a short holiday at the Caithness home of her friends Commander and Lady Doris Vyner, not long after the King's death, that she heard about the proposed demolition of Barrogill Castle, built four hundred years previously by the Earl of Caithness. Spontaneously she deplored its threatened passing, and decided to acquire it as much as an act of historical and architectural preservation (the Castle has a barrel-vaulted ceiling) as for herself. A long period of restoration followed: the interiors were renovated and filled with furniture which she personally collected almost piece by piece, the facilities were modernised, and the gardens gradually persuaded into shape with the front lawn sporting two trees which King Edward VII and Queen Alexandra, then Prince and Princess of Wales, had planted in the 1870's.

The Queen Mother restored not only the building but also its original name, the Castle of Mey. And despite – perhaps because of – its isolated position on the coldest of north-east coasts, it has become her place of pilgrimage since she first moved in at the end of October 1955. Once upon a time she used to spend two or three short holidays a year there, but now restricts herself to a single visit, usually in the company of half a

dozen friends, during the few weeks of the summer when everything is at its best. The woods to the front of the Castle are in full leaf, bounded by the Thurso river where she once fished for salmon; the coastal views of the Pentland Firth to the rear are clear, with distant vistas of the Orkneys on the finest days; and the weather allows her to take a breezy consitutional over the cliffs or on the beaches, where she might collect shells for the cosy rooms of the house itself. Within the four high brick walls shelters the archetypal cottage garden – a large-scale affair stretching over two acres – where everything

from soft fruits to herbs, and begonias to clematis, are reared and nursed into maturity ready for her annual visit. The garden is now open briefly to the public who can see for themselves the profusion of snapdragon and sweet pea, gooseberry and geranium, apple and artichoke – a rich pattern of colour and ripeness amid the bleak, peaty landscape.

Although, now in her eighties, the Queen Mother keeps a lighter engagement book than previously, her years of widowhood have never wilfully been devoid of a programme of official duty. Holidays have, as is the royal wont, been sufficiently lengthy to sustain her through the months of heavy commitments but barring accidents, those schedules have always been scrupulously attended to. "Work," she is said to have drummed into her two daughters during their childhood, "is the rent you pay for life," and even now she tries to eke out her hundred or so public engagements per year to favour as many as possible of the three hundred organisations who rely on her patronage. It takes no mathematician to appreciate that this is no easy task, particularly as the Queen Mother, despite her dislike of anniversaries and undue respect for precedent, likes to be seen to be especially associated with specific annual events. January will for instance see her taking

A subdued celebration for the Queen Mother, seen (opposite page) leaving St Paul's Cathedral with Prince Charles, Princess Anne and their spouses after the service to commemorate the end of hostilities in the Falklands, in July 1982. This was the first public engagement for the Princess of Wales since Prince William's birth a month earlier. Another link with Prince Charles characterised the Queen Mother's visit aboard the Thames sailing barge Dannebrog at St Katherine's Dock in London, also in July. The yacht is the team base of the Operation Drake Fellowship which, inaugurated under Prince Charles' auspices in the 1970s, offers training courses to unemployed school-leavers in Britain's urban areas.

tea with the ladies of the Women's Institute at West Newton near Sandringham – indeed she often helps to prepare the food, especially if the Queen and Princess Margaret are with her, and rarely comes away without having bought the odd trinket or piece of embroidery worked by one of its members. In February she will attend the King's Lynn Festival of Music and Arts, and in March she revels in the quaint old ceremony of distributing the shamrocks to the Irish Guards on St Patrick's Day, wherever one of their battalions may be stationed. This is good fun as much as anything – "One for you – and one for me" ran one recent headline showing the Queen Mother and the battalion commanding officer merrily pinning clumps of shamrock on each other in mutual admiration. April invariably sees the Queen Mother enjoying the country air at the Duke of Beaufort's Badminton estate in Gloucestershire. She has attended almost every year's three-day eventing tournament since its inception in 1949, and the Beauforts – the Duchess is a niece of Queen Mary – play host to her for four days, as they do in March when she stays there in order to attend the Cheltenham race festival each year. Those visits provide a reminder of the five wonderful years Queen Mary spent there during the war, when she formed such close and informal ties with the staff and local people. "I *have* enjoyed myself here," she said on leaving in 1945. "Here I've been anybody to everybody, and now I shall have to start being Queen Mary all over again!"

The Queen Mother's habitual May engagement is, predictably, the Chelsea Flower Show, one of the many expressions of her passionate interest in and knowledge of flowers and gardens. Another such annual

example comes usually in June when, as long-standing Patron of the London Gardens Society, she spends an afternoon being escorted around the gardens of ordinary folk in Greater London, whose efforts over the past year have won prizes in the Society's annual competition. This is a pleasantly relaxed and relaxing engagement, with the Queen Mother talking knowledgeably about her favourite subject, the skills of which – despite now being a "second hand" gardener – she learned from her mother. The horticultural world's greatest tribute to her – the Elizabeth of Glamis rose, developed by Sam McGready – evidences her interest and their appreciation. In this she

An informal outdoor royal birthday gathering to which all were welcome: these two youngsters (top) were among the hundreds of people who waited for a glimpse of the Queen Mother outside Clarence House (above) on the morning of her 82nd birthday, just before attending Prince William's Christening. Predictably the single marigold was as acceptable as any official bouquet. A single rose, too, (left) for the Queen Mother during her 1982 visit to London Gardens – she is most at home against this typical backdrop of well-tended colourful blooms in natural settings (opposite page).

compares well with the Queen, who has admitted that "I am not particularly renowned for my green fingers."

In June or July the Queen Mother goes on tour of her own five ports – the Cinque Ports on the south-east coast of England, of which she became the 160th Lord Warden, succeeding the late Sir Robert Menzies, in 1978. This ancient office, stemming from the days when the ports

The Christening of Prince William at Buckingham Palace meant more to the Queen Mother than a great family occasion: it focused upon the unsuspecting child born to be the eventual successor to her husband – his great grandfather King George VI. Prince Charles was canny enough to mark a further significance – the link between Prince William's birth and the Victorian era – by choosing the Queen Mother's 82nd birthday (4th August 1982) for the Christening.

constituted Britain's first line of defence in the event of invasion, is coupled with that of Constable of Dover Castle, and it was on a wet, windy August day in 1979 that she went to Dover to be installed. There was a special hallowing service at the Church of St Mary in Castro, within the Castle precincts, then a stately carriage drive in – appropriately enough – the Scottish State Coach with Prince Edward, Viscount Linley and Lady Sarah Armstrong-Jones into the town. Here, in a candy-striped marquee in the grounds of Dover College she assumed office, gravely promising to maintain its traditions and obligations, yet twinkling with

thought, to all the traditional privileges. She has visited the ports annually ever since, attending all sorts of formalities from the launching of boats to the Hastings winkle ceremony! Eleanor Roosevelt, in one of her few reservations about the Queen Mother, thought that "she was a little self-consciously regal" in 1939, but if there was a deliberate pose, it was almost certainly one which the American public expected, and which Her Majesty knew they expected, "This one's always a hit," said another American in 1954, using the language of stardom with which British royalty is often blessed in the States, and the radio and news

humour as she referred to the break of tradition which had resulted in her appointment as the first woman to hold it, and again at the thought that she might have to pay for the disposal and burial of any whales washed up on the port's beaches – "a troublesome rider," she

A tradition for sixty years is the Royal Family's attendance at the annual Braemar Games. 1982 (these pages) was no less a family occasion than others, with the Princess of Wales enjoying her second visit (above) and the Queen providing some family fun (top) during the presentation of prizes.

journalist Godfrey Talbot has confirmed that "she thrives on public scrutiny." A less appreciative remark came from the pen of the republican Willie Hamilton MP who, as a prelude to one of his many scathing attacks on the Queen Mother's Civil List allowance, opined that "if a personal public image is the thing to cultivate today, then the Queen Mother is the best of gardeners." Neatly put, but clearly you can't please them all. The Canadians were pleased to see her in 1939 when, we are told, she got out of bed during a journey on the blue and silver train, put on her dressing gown and a tiara, and waved from the observation platform to a crowd of well wishers who had waited through the night to see her; Zulus were equally delighted that on a boiling hot day in 1947

she insisted on dressing in full formal evening gown with tiara and jewels because "this is how they would expect me to look, and they'd know it was me;" even the most *blasé* débutantes must have been impressed when, in 1951, she revived the old pre-war custom by which they were presented individually to the sovereign, because she guessed that they would like to feel they had personally met their host and hostess.
But surely the most popular illustration of the Queen Mother's willingness to "go on public display" is the annual (or almost annual) appearance she makes, and has made since her seventieth birthday, on the narrow, flower-bedecked balcony of Clarence House, to acknowledge the cheers and good wishes of a crowd, now

growing larger by the year, who wait for much of the morning of 4th August to wish her Happy Birthday. Her appearance is usually only brief, though a few years ago it was extended to include a walk to the house's outer gate where the sight of small children thrusting flowers and presents into her hands is now familiar. The practice is now so well established – she has failed to appear only once recently, and that was in the wake of the Prince and Princess of Wales' wedding just six days before her 81st birthday – that it is the only thing which keeps her from beginning her summer holiday first at Sandringham, where her husband was born and died, and then in Scotland. Part of that aptitude for the very public side of her existence is

The Queen Mother arriving (above) for the Royal Variety Performance at the Theatre Royal, Drury Lane in November 1982. On this occasion she was accompanied by her grand-daughter Lady Sarah Armstrong-Jones, and by her niece Princess Alexandra and the Hon. Angus Ogilvy. (Left and above left) the same month, she paid her annual visit to the Royal College of Music in London - her last engagement before the celebrated fishbone incident which put her in hospital for several days. In December the Queen Mother, following Princess Michael's example the year before, presented awards to 1982's Children of Courage at Westminster Abbey – this was the ninth such ceremony since the awards were first inaugurated.

reflected in the Queen Mother's clothes, something for which, like all other elements of her public appearance, she is more than prepared to make time. Despite the death a few years ago of Norman Hartnell, (he used, incidentally, to send her red roses every birthday – the number according to her age – but he stopped increasing the size of the bouquet after she reached six dozen years!) the Queen Mother still looks to his London fashion house for most of her day clothes. Although in the highly fashion-conscious days before the last war she was a sophisticated dresser – "I have never seen her looking so beautiful," wrote Chips Channon in 1939. "She was dressed to perfection" – she has always avoided any risk of artificiality without losing the essential elegance on formal or semi-formal occasions. Her style has for many years been distinctive rather then exciting, safe rather than adventurous – "Why should I not be known for my style of dressing?" she recently asked. But, with her straightish lines and the pastel or light colours which, she feels, make it easier for the public to pick her out, she always looks becoming. She prefers not to wear thick,

heavy clothes except for the occasional raw day at Badminton or the races; she adores pure silk when it is appropriate, and persists, with unquestionable success, in wearing upon her petite, still dainty feet those small high-heeled shoes and slingbacks which help to raise her an inch or two above her natural height of five feet two inches. Her clothes are designed as a result of private fittings and discussions at Clarence House, where a Hartnell advisor, along with a tailor and dressmaker, spend about an hour each fortnight thumbing through pattern books and pads of materials. The Queen Mother makes her own decisions, based on the suggestions of her visitors, and what gratifies them most is that "although she has had thousands of outfits in her time she always shows undiminished interest in the one you are making." Although many of her clothes are of turquoise or aquamarine, she is not keen on wearing green which she considers unlucky. King George VI never liked it, and she hardly ever wore it again after his death. It has always been thought that Prince Charles is the Queen Mother's favourite grandson, so

It was all smiles on 28th October 1982 when the Queen Mother attended the reception at the Press Club, on the very day of its centenary. As the first honorary lady member of the Club she was of course the prime candidate for the

position of cutter of the centenary cake (above) and she brandished a dangerously broad knife as a playful symbol of possible retributions for pressmen who fall foul of royal displeasure. The Press Club likes to keep things in the family of course,

and chose the occasion to ask the Queen Mother to unveil a portrait of her grandson, the Prince of Wales, who is the Club's patron (opposite page, top right). The portrait, by Henry Mee, now hangs in the Club's dining room, next to one of the Duke

of Edinburgh. Among those presented was John Gerard, editor of the UK Press Gazette, whose glasses collapsed just as he was being introduced. "What you need," said the Queen Mother, "is a paper clip".

his marriage to the charming Lady Diana Spencer must have been particularly welcome to her.

In the wake of the enormous publicity engendered by their wedding in July 1981, the Queen Mother made little of her 81st birthday that August. Her 82nd however more than made up for that. In June 1982, the Princess of Wales had given birth to a healthy baby boy, Prince William, whose reign will, God willing, take the fascinating story of Britain's Royal Family into the second half of the 21st century. It was the most considerate expression of Prince Charles' sense of history and appreciation of all he owes to his grandmother that he should

have chosen her 82nd birthday – 4th August 1982 – for the christening of his six week old son. Oddly, and unexpectedly, there was no George or Albert in the child's quartet of names – William Arthur Philip Louis – which were pronounced over him as water from the River Jordan was spooned over him, but the Queen Mother's presence provided the links with the past which Prince Charles was anxious to secure and have recorded. Just as Queen Mary had held him on her knee in 1948, so Queen Elizabeth the Queen Mother, a visible connection between two vastly different eras, cradled the future King in her lap. Prince William's sense of occasion was not quite

Almost every member of the Royal Family makes a point of attending, in some way or other, the festivals and ceremonies of remembrance. For the Queen Mother in particular, some of whose brothers, nephews and cousins were killed, wounded or taken prisoner during the two World Wars, these traditional national commemorations are more than mere ceremonial.

(Overleaf) the Royal Family turned out in force for Ascot 1983.

as well developed: he had obviously become hungry during the ceremony, and the Queen Mother's only comment as she withstood his vocal assaults on her was, "Well, at least he's got a good pair of lungs."

For a member of the Royal Family living, as it were, on her own and with a diary of engagements now averaging less than two a week, it seems strange, and to some, wrong that she should benefit from the Civil List to the tune of £321,000 per year, almost double Prince Philip's allowance and almost three times those of Princess Anne or Princess Margaret. The answer lies in the Queen Mother's unique rank as widow of a sovereign, which entitles her to a home, a staff and a way of life close to what she would have enjoyed as the King's consort. Consequently, she has a staff of over three dozen – some of whom are on duty part time, and many of whom are unpaid. The unsalaried members of her household are usually old friends holding honorary appointments after many years of faithful service, and her

ladies-in-waiting (called Women of the Bedchamber if they attend her on day to day occasions, and Ladies of the Bedchamber if on ceremonial duties) go on and off duty in rota, each "shift" lasting from four to six weeks. Between them they keep Clarence House running efficiently both as an administrative enterprise geared to the necessities of the Queen Mother's official life, and as a home, offering her the comforts to which she has become accustomed.

For all that efficiency, she has for many years been indulgently believed to be notoriously unpunctual. This is normally an

unforgiveable weakness in any member of the Royal Family, whose schedules are worked out months in advance and usually timed to the minute. Queen Victoria and Queen Mary were both models of punctuality – the latter was even born on the very day she was expected – but the Queen Mother, like Queen Alexandra who was, it is said, late for her own Coronation, tends to let the minutes slip by. What Cecil Beeton had praised as her movements "in slow motion" can evidently have disadvantages. There is a belief that she has a notice on her

desk saying in large capital letters DO IT NOW, and an equally widespread counter belief that she has never thought it to have had the slightest effect on her. In effect, any lack of punctuality is more often than not of the type which can always be embraced with cheerfulness, namely that which springs from a consuming interest in whom she is meeting, and what she is doing. It is rarely her arrivals that are late – it is the getting away again.

That this tolerable weakness still exists today, when her advanced years if nothing else would give her every excuse for making short work of her official duties, is a measure of the importance she attaches to continuing that work while she has the power to do so. Her few illnesses, especially in recent years, have been trivial indeed – the occasional chill and bout of 'flu, the leg ulcer which almost kept her away from the Prince of Wales' wedding in 1981, but which just healed in time, the brief cold which prevented her from joining the rest of her family for the customary Christmas Day Morning Service at St George's Chapel Windsor Castle – all bear satisfactory comparison with those lengthy

indispositions which interrupted her honeymoon in 1923, kept her out of action at the time of the death of King George V and again at the Accession of King George VI, or postponed a tour or two in the mid 1960s. Her little brush with the fishbone in November 1982 accentuated her eagerness not to let small matters get in the way of what she clearly enjoys – a job of work which, in its own way and following her own lights, adds to the quality of an all too mundane life today. The "touch of the twinkle which she keeps for old friends" is now a regular accompaniment to even the most ordinary of duties. It is a

trait by which her family have been greatly influenced over the years and which has undoubtedly helped to modernise the monarchy while keeping her young both in spirit and in the esteem of her daughter's subjects. That, in a cynical age when true esteem is hard to come by, is no mean achievement and is ample reward for the long life of dedication, wisdom and inspiration which Queen Elizabeth the Queen Mother has put at the service of her country and of the family whose duty it is in perpetuity to reign over it.

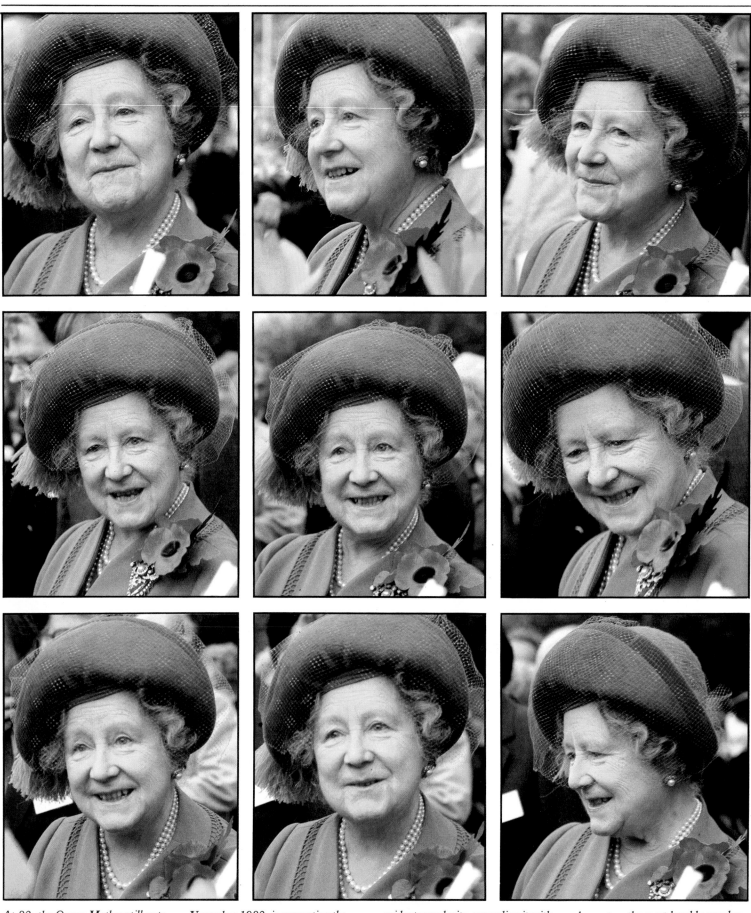

At 82, the Queen Mother still puts everything into her public appearances. At Hyde Park in November 1982, inaugurating the Beautiful Britain campaign she was as animated as ever, revelling in her evident popularity, rewarding it with the concern, kindness and sheer fun which, for sixty years, have marked her out as the most lovable member of the Royal Family.